THE DEPARTMENT OF HOMELAND SECURITY'S PROPOSED REGULATIONS REFORMING THE INVESTOR VISA PROGRAM

HEARING

BEFORE THE

COMMITTEE ON THE JUDICIARY
HOUSE OF REPRESENTATIVES

ONE HUNDRED FIFTEENTH CONGRESS

FIRST SESSION

MARCH 8, 2017

Serial No. 115–4

Printed for the use of the Committee on the Judiciary

Available via the World Wide Web: http://judiciary.house.gov

U.S. GOVERNMENT PUBLISHING OFFICE

24–970   WASHINGTON : 2017

For sale by the Superintendent of Documents, U.S. Government Publishing Office
Internet: bookstore.gpo.gov   Phone: toll free (866) 512–1800; DC area (202) 512–1800
Fax: (202) 512–2104   Mail: Stop IDCC, Washington, DC 20402–0001

COMMITTEE ON THE JUDICIARY

BOB GOODLATTE, Virginia, *Chairman*

F. JAMES SENSENBRENNER, JR.,
  Wisconsin
LAMAR SMITH, Texas
STEVE CHABOT, Ohio
DARRELL E. ISSA, California
STEVE KING, Iowa
TRENT FRANKS, Arizona
LOUIE GOHMERT, Texas
JIM JORDAN, Ohio
TED POE, Texas
JASON CHAFFETZ, Utah
TOM MARINO, Pennsylvania
TREY GOWDY, South Carolina
RAUL LABRADOR, Idaho
BLAKE FARENTHOLD, Texas
DOUG COLLINS, Georgia
RON DeSANTIS, Florida
KEN BUCK, Colorado
JOHN RATCLIFFE, Texas
MARTHA ROBY, Alabama
MATT GAETZ, Florida
MIKE JOHNSON, Louisiana
ANDY BIGGS, Arizona

JOHN CONYERS, JR., Michigan
JERROLD NADLER, New York
ZOE LOFGREN, California
SHEILA JACKSON LEE, Texas
STEVE COHEN, Tennessee
HENRY C. "HANK" JOHNSON, JR., Georgia
THEODORE E. DEUTCH, Florida
LUIS V. GUTIÉRREZ, Illinois
KAREN BASS, California
CEDRIC L. RICHMOND, Louisiana
HAKEEM S. JEFFRIES, New York
DAVID CICILLINE, Rhode Island
ERIC SWALWELL, California
TED LIEU, California
JAMIE RASKIN, Maryland
PRAMILA JAYAPAL, Washington
BRAD SCHNEIDER, Illinois

SHELLEY HUSBAND, *Chief of Staff and General Counsel*
PERRY APELBAUM, *Minority Staff Director and Chief Counsel*

CONTENTS

MARCH 8, 2017

OPENING STATEMENTS

OFFICIAL HEARING RECORD

MATERIAL SUBMITTED FOR THE RECORD

Statement submitted by the Honorable Sheila Jackson Lee, Texas, Committee on the Judiciary. This material is available at the Committee and can be accessed on the committee repository at:

   http://docs.house.gov/meetings/JU/JU00/20170308/105660/HHRG-115-JU00-20170308-SD002.pdf.

THE DEPARTMENT OF HOMELAND SECURITY'S PROPOSED REGULATIONS REFORMING THE INVESTOR VISA PROGRAM

WEDNESDAY, MARCH 8, 2017

House of Representatives,

Committee on the Judiciary,

Washington, DC.

The committee met, pursuant to call, at 10:10 a.m., in Room 2141, Rayburn House Office Building, Hon. Bob Goodlatte (chairman of the committee) presiding.

Present: Representatives Goodlatte, Sensenbrenner, Chabot, Issa, King, Gohmert, Jordan, Poe, Marino, Gowdy, Labrador, Buck, Gaetz, Johnson of Louisiana, Biggs, Conyers, Nadler, Lofgren, Jackson Lee, Deutch, Cicilline, Lieu, Jayapal, and Schneider.

Staff Present: Shelley Husband, Staff Director; Branden Ritchie, Deputy Staff Director; Zach Somers, Parliamentarian and General Counsel; George Fishman, Counsel, Subcommittee on Immigration and Border Security; Danielle Brown, Minority Parliamentarian and Chief Legislative Counsel; David Shahoulian, Minority Chief Counsel, Subcommittee on Immigration and Border Security; Veronica Eligan, Minority Professional Staff Member; and Joseph Ehrenkrantz, Minority Legislative Aide.

Chairman GOODLATTE. We welcome everyone to this morning's hearing on "The Department of Homeland Security's Proposed Regulations Reforming the Investor Visa Program."

We will begin today by recognizing our first panel of witnesses for their statements. After they have concluded, I will recognize myself and the ranking member for our opening statements.

The Honorable Chuck Grassley is a United States Senator from Iowa, where he has been a leader in shaping legislation to expand the economic opportunities for individuals, families, and communities. Senator Grassley serves as chairman of the Senate Committee on the Judiciary. He also serves as a senior member of the Senate Committee on the Budget and on the Senate Committee on Agriculture. Senator Grassley was previously chairman of the Committee on Finance.

The Honorable Patrick Leahy is ranked first in seniority in the United States Senate. Senator Leahy is the vice chair of the Senate Appropriations Committee. He is the senior-most member of the Senate Judiciary Committee and of the Senate Agriculture Committee. Senator Leahy is the ranking member of the Appropriations

Subcommittee on State Department, Foreign Operations, and Related Programs.

I would ask each witness to summarize his or her testimony in 5 minutes or less. To help you stay within that time, there is timing light on your table. When the light switches from green to yellow—well, you guys know how this works, even though you are in the Senate.

We welcome both of you. We welcome both of you, and we will begin by recognizing Chairman Grassley. Welcome.

STATEMENT OF THE HON. CHUCK GRASSLEY, A UNITED STATES SENATOR FROM THE STATE OF IOWA

Senator GRASSLEY. Chairman Goodlatte, Ranking Member Conyers, and all the members of this very good committee, thank you very much for inviting me to testify about the EB–5 investor visa program. Senator Leahy and I have longstanding concerns with the regional center program. We have worked together for years to address this program's rampant waste, fraud, and abuse.

In 1990, Congress created the EB–5 program. The goal was to create new employment opportunities for American workers. A mere 2 years later, Congress established a pilot program which allowed investors to pool their investments in regional centers. The theory was simple: by allocating investors to pool their funds, greater investment would occur, and jobs for American workers would flourish.

Twenty-five years later, this pilot program still exists, but it is deeply flawed and has strayed very much from its original intent. There are many problems with the regional center program, but let me mention just a few of the worst.

Jobs created are not direct and verifiable jobs. They, instead, are indirect and based on vague estimates and economic modeling. A foreign national is allowed to count all jobs created by a project when obtaining their green card. This is even if EB–5 money is only a mere fraction of total investment. Investment funds are not adequately vetted, and there are no prohibitions against foreign governments owning or operating regional centers. Even more concerning, background checks aren't required for anyone associated with regional centers. This raises serious questions about whether foreign governments are selling U.S. green cards to their citizens. Regional centers gerrymander targeted employment areas and the boundaries therein to encompass economically distressed areas in order to come in at a lower investment level.

This is an issue because the jobs created aren't actually created in those areas, and the projects aren't actually in those areas. The problem is made worse by the fact that every targeted employment area designation is just simply rubber stamped.

Finally, and perhaps the most frustrating, the minimum investment level hasn't been raised in 25 years. I could keep going on about many abuses. With this in mind, I believe that either the regional center program should be completely overhauled and reformed, or it should expire. The American people deserve better than what we are getting out of this program.

Senator Leahy and I have tried to work in a bicameral and bipartisan way to enact real EB reforms. Last year, the Senate Judiciary Committee held two hearings alone on this subject, and this committee we are before now held another. We heard from local leaders and associations representing workers in regional centers. We listened to the academics and government officials. We received feedback from many industries as well as immigration and security attorneys. After painstaking negotiations and concessions by almost every stakeholder, some of us more than others, we reached consensus and would reauthorize that program for 6 years. Unfortunately, this wasn't acceptable to all parties. Instead of addressing the program's waste, fraud, and abuse, Congress merely reauthorized, as you know.

Nothing better supports the need for serious reform than the work that Chairman Chaffetz and I have done to draw attention to the program's very real national concerns. We have sent several letters and conducted transcribed interviews with key players of an interagency working group to assess just how rampant fraud and abuse are in the program.

This working group made several recommendations, the most compelling of which was to sunset the regional center model due to crippling fraud, national security vulnerabilities.

I also want to take a moment to address the reforms proposed by the Obama administration. Earlier this year, former Homeland Security Secretary Johnson published proposed rule changes to the regional center, the program, that would stop gerrymandering and increase investment levels. I strongly support these changes. They are a vital first step—but just a first step—to returning the program to its original intent, creating new employment for American workers and infusing capital into the distressed rural areas.

When I met Secretary Kelly before his confirmation, I emphasized the importance of those rules, and he seemed favorable to them. I want to continue working with my colleagues of both Chambers and both parties to reform the program. I look forward especially to working with you, Chairman Goodlatte and Ranking Member Conyers, and hopefully the Trump administration in the coming months on legislation that is serious and substantial.

Thank you for receiving my testimony.

[Senator Grassley's written statement is available at the Committee or on the committee repository at: *http://docs.house.gov/ meetings/JU/JU00/20170308/105660/HHRG-115-JU00-Wstate-GrassleyC-20170308.pdf*]

Chairman GOODLATTE. Thank you, Senator Grassley. Senator Leahy, welcome.

STATEMENT OF THE HON. PATRICK J. LEAHY, A UNITED STATES SENATOR FROM THE STATE OF VERMONT

Senator LEAHY. Thank you, Mr. Chairman and Ranking Member Conyers. I appreciate being here with my good friend Chairman Grassley.

You know, the last several years, as Senator Grassley said, we worked together across the aisle. We got to work across the Capitol, as you know, to try to bring overdue reforms to the EB–5 regional center program. The EB–5 program that I once championed seems like a distant memory. That program was designed to bring jobs to underserved rural and urban communities. And for some time, it did just that, but the program has strayed from these goals, and it is a magnet for fraud. Security violations are common, and the incentives that Congress created to promote investment in distressed areas have become obsolete due to economic gerrymandering. Only 3 percent of EB–5 investors now invest in rural areas, 3 percent. I am representing a State that has a lot of rural areas. I note that number.

Less than 10 percent invest in true high-unemployment areas. Almost every EB–5 project uses gerrymandering to qualify as distressed. I will give you an example: a luxury hotel in Beverly Hills uses gerrymandering to claim it is located in a distressed community, one of the wealthiest communities in America. But the fact that this type of abuse represents almost 90 percent of the entire EB–5 program is appalling. I am told a number of these luxury developments would be pursued whether they had EB–5 financing or not. So it casts real doubt on whether this is creating any jobs at all.

In my home State of Vermont, EB–5 has been used in areas it would not otherwise have been able to attract significant investment. But even in Vermont, experience has clearly shown the need for the reforms and the transparency—transparency, which is so important—that we are trying to achieve.

In our State, the news organization Vermont Digger has dug deeply, if you will excuse the pun, to reveal the need for broad reforms. Yet, for some developers, any change to the status quo is a threat to their bottom line. And, unfortunately, some in our leadership have allowed a couple of powerful developers who exploit this program's flaws to derail critical reform. That is unacceptable. The worst abusers of a government program should not be given veto power over its reform.

Now, the Department of Homeland Security's proposed rules represent a significant step forward. I agree with Senator Grassley. When we asked then Secretary Jeh Johnson over a year ago to do all he could do to improve the EB–5 program, he worked at that, and I commend him for that. By increasing investment amounts, reining in abusive gerrymandering practices, these changes will end some of the most egregious abuses. Investors will be afforded greater flexibility when circumstances changed through no fault of their own, which is going to bring additional fairness to the program. But the Trump administration is going to have to make sure these are implemented and improved.

And, Chairman Goodlatte and my friend Chairman Grassley, I thank you for shining a spotlight on this issue. You can't let these proposed rules be diluted or discarded, because this thing will just spin out of control. I still believe, as did Secretary Johnson, the EB–5's many problems ultimately demand a legislative solution. I think we need that. I remain committed to doing more to protect investors to root out fraud within the program, increasing fraud investigations, requiring additional oversight.

Chairman Grassley and I will soon reintroduce our legislation that would do just that. It is my hope that serious reforms proposed in new rules would lead to these broader improvements. But I look forward to working with all of you on this committee as well as on ours to make sure the EB–5 program, again, serves the rural and poor urban communities that Congress intended.

Thank you very much.

[Senator Leahy's written statement is available at the Committee or on the committee repository at: *http://docs.house.gov/meetings/JU/JU00/20170308/105660/HHRG-115-JU00-Wstate-LeahyP-20170308.pdf*]

Chairman GOODLATTE. Thank you, Senator Leahy.

I want to thank both of you for your insights into this program and these important regulatory reforms. And as is our custom, we will not have a round of questioning for you. And I know you have other matters to attend to. So thank you very much, and we will at this time excuse both of you.

Senator LEAHY. Thank you. Good to see you.

Chairman GOODLATTE. I will now recognize myself for an opening statement.

In 1990, Congress created the investment visa program in order to bring entrepreneurial talent to the United States, create new jobs, and infuse new capital into our economy, especially in hard-hit rural and depressed areas. Unfortunately, over the years, the program has strayed further and further from Congress' intent and has seen its reputation repeatedly tarnished by scandal.

For the past year and a half, I have worked collaboratively with Ranking Member Conyers, Representative Issa, and Senators Grassley and Leahy to reform the program and set it on a solid foundation.

Currently, aliens must invest $1 million unless they invest in projects in rural or high-unemployment areas, in which case they can invest half of this amount. These levels have remained untouched since 1990, a quarter century ago, never adjusted for inflation or any other factor. As a result, the real value of each investment has fallen by half. Almost all visas now go to aliens investing at the lower level, meant for rural and poor areas, even when the resulting projects are built in prosperous areas. Regional centers have discovered that they can duct tape together ritzy, high-rent districts with distant depressed zones in order that the combined area magically meets the high-unemployment test. The Government Accountability Office found that 12 percent of projects qualifying as high-unemployment TEAs, in fact, taped together over 100 disparate census tracts. The GAO also found that more than three-quarters of projects in supposedly high-unemployment areas are actually physically located in places with unemployment rates from zero to 6 percent.

This gerrymandering takes place to access cheap capital. Aliens don't care about their rate of return as much as they do procuring green cards. Real estate experts at New York University have concluded that, quote: "Projects in even the most affluent areas are able to routinely qualify for the discounted investment. This gerrymandering renders the two-level investment threshold meaningless, and foreign investors flock to invest in luxury projects," end quote.

For example, here is Hudson Yards, a Manhattan mega development that purchased a 4-page spread in the 800-page September issue of Vogue. Based on Vogue's rack rate, the ad cost Hudson

Yards about $800,000. It boasts that Hudson Yards will include some of the tallest and grandest towers in the city. Inside, soaring ceilings, walls of glass, and ingenious details reflect the highest standards in the residential market. Boasting a collection of restaurants curated by world-renowned chef Thomas Keller, Hudson Yards is poised to become the city's most unique and exciting dining destination. A unique combination of luxury retailers and independent boutiques is being curated. You can rejuvenate in the innovative luxury spa, and on and on.

At the Yard's first condominium project, condos will start at around $1.9 million for 843 square feet and rise to $32 million for the two penthouses. Perhaps in recognition of the huge success of HGTV's show, Tiny Houses, the real deal, a New York real estate journal states that 200 of the total 285 market-rate condos are priced at 7 million—at below $7 million. The move is reflective of a general drift in the market toward smaller homes at less ostentatious prices. Things must be tough all over.

Of course, Hudson Yards is marketing investor visas for $500,000.

Projects in affluent areas will always be able to compete for foreign investors. Even if aliens have to invest more, they prefer the lower risk of the investments and their prestigious ZIP Codes. However, if Congress is going to be granting a path to citizenship, we have every right to ensure that a healthy percentage of investments be in rural and depressed areas, as Congress originally intended.

I have been one of the most vocal opponents of the Obama administration's executive overreach. However, for the past quarter century, both Democratic and Republican administrations have engaged in executive underreach when it comes to the investor visa program. Congress gave the administration explicit statutory authority to raise the minimum investment amounts. Congress gave the administration the power to determine for itself which areas qualify as depressed rather than simply delegating away this authority. And, yet, no administration acted until January.

In one of his last acts, Secretary of Homeland Security Jeh Johnson commendably issued proposed regulations that deliver long overdue reform. The regulations proposed to raise the minimum investment amount to $1.8 million. While this is higher than what I was willing to accept last year, in the spirit of compromise, it is eminently justifiable, merely accounting for inflation over the past quarter century and far lower than the investment amount required by our international competitors. The regulations would also raise the minimum investment amount for rural and high-unemployment areas to $1.35 million and effectively end gerrymandering by defining a high-unemployment area as the census tract or tracts in which a project is principally doing business and, at the discretion of the regional center, any or all census tracts directly adjacent to the project tract, a concept I proposed 2 years ago. These regulations deserve to be issued in final form, and I urge the Trump administration to do so. They will enable the investor visa program to become a turbo-charged engine for economic growth. If, however, the regulations are not finalized and the program remains in disrepair, I am not sure that it deserves to continue.

I look forward to hearing from today's further witnesses. And I am now pleased to recognize the ranking member, the gentleman from Michigan, Mr. Conyers, for his opening statement.

Mr. CONYERS. Thank you, Chairman Goodlatte, for what I agree is a very comprehensive statement.

Members of the committee, last Congress, I had the honor of working with Chairman Grassley and Senator Leahy in an effort to reform the EB–5 investor visa program. While the proposed Department of Homeland Security regulations would go a long way toward addressing many of our longstanding and serious concerns with the program, there is no substitute to a meaningful legislative solution.

I remain confident that we can accomplish these important legislative reforms this Congress, and I look forward to working with you on this, Chairman Goodlatte.

I have taken a particular interest in the EB–5 investor visa program because I believe it has drifted far from the program initially envisioned by Congress. As a result, the communities that need investment the most, specifically rural and distressed urban areas, struggle to benefit from the program and are unfairly placed in direct competition with the developed, affluent areas. We have already heard some examples of that.

When Congress established the EB–5 investor visa program in 1990, the intention was to create jobs for American citizens and to bring new investment capital to the United States. To help encourage investment in job creation in rural or high-unemployment areas, the EB–5 program offered a reduced investment level of $500,000 for projects in designated target employment areas.

However, as reported by the GAO, academics, Wall Street Journal, and other news sources, the vast majority of the EB–5 investment funds are going to projects in some of America's wealthiest corridors. They qualify as TEAs, or economically distressed, only by aggregating census tracts across many miles, sometimes across State lines, and often across natural boundaries, such as rivers.

I call it economic gerrymandering. This practice has been criticized by the Leadership Conference on Civil Rights, noting that the EB–5 regional center program has dramatically deviated from its original purpose to spur job creation and development in rural and high-unemployment areas.

Steering investments to projects in our cities' well-to-do neighborhoods comes at the expense of EB–5 funds for urban and rural communities. According to the Center for American Progress, the congressional district that I represent, for instance, I am sorry to say, is the second most impoverished district in the United States. I am pleased to say that, under the Obama administration, our economic environment began to improve. It is slow, and we have a long way to go, but for those Americans living in my city of Detroit and in many other cities across the country, manipulation of targeted employment areas has diverted a potential source of jobs and neighborhood improvement away from those that it was originally intended to help.

The Department of Homeland Security's proposed rules make a number of important reforms. First, the rules would raise the higher investment level to adjust for inflation from $1 million to $1.8

million and would raise the lower investment amount from $500,000 to $1.35 million.

Secondly, the rules would reduce the difference between the statutory and targeted employment area investment levels and would allow for conforming adjustments based on inflation beginning 5 years from the effective date.

And, lastly, the rules would significantly rein in manipulation of targeted employment areas. I am encouraged by this development from the Department of Homeland Security and consider the proposed rulemakings as movement in the right direction. But I must reiterate: to achieve the necessary reforms to the EB–5 program, there is no substitute to a meaningful legislative solution. And absent significant reform, either regulatory or legislative, I will not be able to support continued authorization of this program.

And so, in closing, I want to thank the witnesses for their willingness to appear before our committee. I look forward to an open debate about the proposed regulations and the future of this valuable program, the EB–5 program.

Thank you, Mr. Chairman. I yield back.

Chairman GOODLATTE. Thank you, Mr. Conyers.

It is now my pleasure to recognize the chairman of the Immigration and Border Security Subcommittee, the gentleman from Wisconsin, Mr. Sensenbrenner, for his opening statement.

Mr. SENSENBRENNER. Thank you very much, Mr. Chairman.

For anyone looking for CliffsNotes on today's hearings, I can summarize it at the onset into two major points that you will hear over and over again.

First, the EB–5 investor visa program brings sustained foreign investment and quality jobs to the U.S. And, second, the program is out of date and has been subject to waste, fraud and abuse. Any time you have a valuable government program that isn't working as well as it should, it is time for reform.

The days of last-minute extensions and continuing resolutions are over. Let me repeat that: no more extensions and CRs. It is time for all parties to come together to the table so that Congress can do the often dirty job of legislating.

The immigrant investor program has made great contributions to our economy. We should not look at its problems today and dismiss it as a failure. Its value was recognized as far back as 1981 by the Select Commission on Immigration and Refugee Policy. The committee concluded that admitting investors into the United States is in the national interest and recommended the creation of a small numerically limited visa program for immigrants who would contribute a substantial amount of investment.

Congress listened and created the EB–5 investor program. Customs and immigration service has reported that since—from its inception in 1990 through 2014, the EB–5 program has created at least 73,730 jobs and generated more than $11.2 billion in investment. We want that capital, and we need those jobs.

But even if I don't like to admit it, the world has changed since we created the program in 1990. The price of a stamp has doubled; so has the price of milk. The number of millionaires in the United States has more than tripled. And the minimum investment in the EB–5 program has not increased by even a nickel.

Other nations with investor visa programs require much larger investments. Australia's investor program requires up to 11 million U.S. dollars. Canada's program requires at least 1.5 million U.S. dollars, in addition to a required personal net worth of over 7 million or more U.S. dollars. And the United Kingdom's investor program requires at least 2.5 million U.S. dollars and millions more for expedited citizenship. There are, of course, some countries that offer cut-rate prices for investment visas, but I for one believe that the value of U.S. citizenship is that higher than any other country in the world, and I think the cost of becoming a U.S. citizen should be fairly valued at way over $500,000.

Demand supports my patriotism because we currently have a 7- to 8-year backlog for the roughly 10,000 investor green cards available each year. I am not an economist, but when demand is that high, it means that the price is too low. An increase in investment amounts would cause considerably more capital to flow into the United States.

Making matters worse, not only are the required investment levels 25 years out of date, but the system has been abused to require even less capital than Congress intended. Congress intended the minimum investment for an EB–5 visa to be $1 million. We then specifically sought to incentivize investments in rural and depressed areas by carving out an exception. In so-called targeted employment areas, Congress lowered the minimum investment amount to $500,000.

These incentives completely failed, however. The targeted boundaries were gerrymandered, and the million-dollar investment level was almost completely ignored. The exception swallowed the rule, and all EB–5 visas are now set at the $500,000 level, even though the majority of capital flows to affluent areas.

Last year, the Department of Homeland Security attempted to address these and other concerns through its rulemaking process. I agree with the intent of DHS' proposed regulations, but Congress, not the administration, is suited to weigh the policy considerations necessary to properly reform the investor visa program.

I thank the chairman for holding this hearing, and I thank Senators Grassley and Leahy for crossing over to the wrong side of the tracks to testify here today.

The four of us, along with Ranking Member Conyers and many other members of this committee, have worked to solve a lot of intractable problems over the years, and I look forward to working with you all to reform the EB–5 program. Thank you.

Chairman GOODLATTE. Thank you, Mr. Sensenbrenner.

The chair is now pleased to recognize the ranking member of the Immigration and Border Security Subcommittee, the gentlewoman from California, Ms. Lofgren, for her opening statement.

Ms. LOFGREN. Thank you, Mr. Chairman.

Created 27 years ago, this EB–5 program is an important investment and job-creation program. It got a slow start, but after the Great Recession in 2008, the program really picked up. When traditional bank lending dried up during the economic crisis, developers turned to the EB–5 program to keep funding projects, and the use of the program has really skyrocketed since then.

Now, I saw a 2017 report from the U.S. Department of Commerce that says in fiscal years 2012 and 2013 alone, the EB–5 program brought in $5.8 billion in capital financing to the United States and was expected to create more than 174,000 jobs. The benefits of this program are on display in the bay area, where I am from. The program has funded a new hotel in the revitalizing San Jose Airport corridor in the 19th Congressional District I represent as well as development in revitalizing Treasure Island. According to investors, these projects would not have happened without EB–5 financing. For example, the hotel in my district was the first one built near the airport in 20 years. And the Treasure Island project includes the island's World's Fair site, which is a California historical landmark and a former military base, which has required significant remediation and redevelopment.

At the same time, there is growing recognition that the program is in need of modernization and reform. As has been mentioned by others, the minimum investment level of 1 million or 500,000 hasn't been updated since the program was created in 1990. And considering the high demand for the program demonstrated by the long and growing backlog of EB–5 petitions, it shows that the U.S. is leaving investment capital on the table by not increasing the investment level.

The program has also come under consideration—criticism with respect to the provisions designed to ensure that EB–5 investments are shared among rural areas and distressed areas. As has been mentioned, my colleagues, the gerrymandering issue is of concern to many. Others worry, however, that excessive tightening of the current conditions would prevent funding of many projects that, although situated in relatively prosperous areas, nonetheless create jobs for workers in nearby distressed areas.

And in the midst of the program's exploding popularity, there is increasing concern about fraud within the program. We have seen reports concerning alleged investment scams, SEC civil violations, and even criminal indictments related to EB–5 projects.

And I will say this, although there has been not yet full consensus on the investment amount and the so-called gerrymandering issue, I do think there is broad consensus on the antifraud provisions no matter what the opinion is on the investment amount.

We do need to reform this program. And as we know, the Department of Homeland Security proposed some changes to reform the program, increasing the threshold amounts and reforming the targeted areas. Whether these proposed changes should be adopted in the final rule—of course, is what we are here to discuss today—or whether the rule should be replaced by legislation, I support increasing the investment threshold to ensure that we are maximizing foreign investments and creating the maximum number of U.S. jobs for workers. But we must also be careful to avoid changes that would reduce the overall investment and, thus, the number of jobs created by the program.

I think we need to look at how we can incent additional development in depressed and rural areas. I do think that we have fallen short there although our intent was clear. But we need to be careful, as we move in that direction, not to impose restrictions that would effectively close off the EB–5 program in large swaths of the country.

These are difficult issues that require careful balancing, and I look forward to hearing from the witnesses today on the right balance.

I would note that, along with this hearing, EB–5 stakeholders are currently submitting comments on the proposed rule for consideration by DHS, which is exactly the way this system should work. By airing proposals and gathering feedback and other data, both the Congress and the Department can weigh competing priorities and hopefully reach the right balance for the good of the country.

I would be remiss if I did not mention that, while this EB–5 hearing is important and a subject deserving of review, I would hope that the committee might also find time to work on the topic of comprehensive immigration reform, something that our country desperately needs.

And, with that, Mr. Chairman, I would yield back the balance of my time.

Chairman GOODLATTE. The chair thanks the gentlewoman.

And I would now invite our second panel members to come forward and take their seats at the witness table.

Thank you. You might want to remain standing since the first thing I am going to do is swear you in.

Welcome to all of you. If you would, please raise your right hand.

Do you each of you solemnly swear that the testimony that you are about to give shall be the truth, the whole truth, and nothing but the truth so help you God?

Thank you.

Let the record reflect that all five witnesses answered in the affirmative.

And you may be seated. Thank you.

Ms. Rebecca Gambler is a Director in the U.S. Government Accountability Office's Homeland Security and Justice Team, where she leads GAO's work on border security, immigration, and elections issues. Ms. Gambler joined GAO in 2002 and has worked on a wide range of issues related to Homeland Security and Justice. Prior to joining the GAO, Ms. Gambler worked at the National Endowment for Democracy's International Forum for Democratic Studies. Ms. Gambler has an M.A. in national security and strategic studies from the United States Naval War College, an M.A. in international relations from Syracuse University, and an M.A. in political science from the University of Toronto. She is a Fulbright fellow to Canada. Ms. Gambler has a B.A. in political science from Messiah College.

Mr. Sam Walls is the president and chief operating officer of Arkansas Capital Corporation, having joined the company in 2003. ACC is a private, nonprofit, economic development company that provides capital to businesses starting or expanding in Arkansas.

In 2012, State leaders approached ACC and asked ACC to consider creating an EB–5 regional center that would serve Arkansas. Consequently, Pine State Regional Center was born. PSRC was approved in 2014, and Mr. Walls serves as its managing director. He has a B.A. from Southern Methodist University in Dallas, Texas, and a J.D. from the William H. Bowen School of Law in Little Rock, Arkansas.

Ms. Angelique Brunner established EB5 Capital in 2007. She splits her time between the company's Washington, D.C., and San Francisco offices providing strategic direction and oversight to EB5 Capital's real estate, marketing, and legal team.

Ms. Brunner serves on the board of directors for Invest In The USA, the national EB–5 industry trade association, and was the inaugural chair of the II USA Policy Committee, which guides the industry's communications with the USCIS and other governmental agencies. Ms. Brunner received her bachelor's degree in public policy from Brown University. She also holds a master's degree in public affairs and a certificate in urban planning from Princeton University's Woodrow Wilson School.

Ms. Dekonti Mends-Cole serves as a director of policy for the Center for Community Progress, which is a nonprofit solely dedicated to transforming blighted and vacant properties into asset-supporting neighborhood vitality. Prior to joining Center for Community Progress in September 2015, Ms. Mends-Cole worked as the deputy director of dispositions for the Detroit Land Bank Authority overseeing disposition, property management, and compliance program.

In addition, she served as a fellow with the White House Strong Cities, Strong Communities initiative embedded in the city of Detroit's law department. Ms. Mends-Cole holds an M.S. from the London School of Economics in urban regeneration and affordable housing, a juris doctor from Georgetown Law Center, and a B.A. from the University of Miami in international studies and economics.

Mr. David North, a fellow of the Center for Immigration Studies, is an authority on immigration policy, specializing on the interaction between immigration and domestic systems, such as education and labor markets. He served in the United States Labor Department as the Assistant for Farm Labor to the U.S. Secretary of Labor and as the Executive Director of President Lyndon Johnson's Cabinet Committee on Mexican-American Affairs. Mr. North received a Fulbright scholarship to attend Victoria University in Wellington, New Zealand, where he earned an M.A. He is also a magna cum laude graduate from Princeton University.

Welcome to all of you. Your timing device is right there in front of you. You have 5 minutes. When it reaches 1 minute remaining, it will turn to yellow. We ask that you summarize and conclude before the red light comes on. Your entire statement will be made a part of the record.

And we will begin with Ms. Gambler.

TESTIMONY OF REBECCA GAMBLER, DIRECTOR, HOMELAND SECURITY AND JUSTICE TEAM, U.S. GOVERNMENT AC-COUNTABILITY OFFICE; SAM WALLS III, MANAGING DIREC-TOR, PINE STATE REGIONAL CENTER; ANGELIQUE BRUN-NER, FOUNDER AND PRESIDENT, EB5 CAPITAL; DEKONTI MENDS-COLE, DIRECTOR OF POLICY, CENTER FOR COMMU-NITY PROGRESS; AND DAVID NORTH, FELLOW, CENTER FOR IMMIGRATION STUDIES

TESTIMONY OF REBECCA GAMBLER

Ms. GAMBLER. Good morning, Chairman Goodlatte, Ranking Member Conyers, and members of the committee. I appreciate the opportunity to testify at today's hearing to discuss GAO's work reviewing the immigrant investor or EB–5 program.

The EB–5 program was established to promote job creation and encourage capital investment in the United States by foreign investors in exchange for a lawful permanent residency and a path to citizenship.

Currently, under the program, immigrant investors are to invest $1 million in a commercial enterprise, or $500,000 if the business is in a targeted employment area, or TEA. A TEA is defined as an area that at the time of investment is either rural or has experienced unemployment of at least 150 percent of the national average rate.

Investments are to result in the creation of at least 10 full-time jobs. Immigrant investors and their eligible dependents receive 2-year conditional green cards. If they meet program requirements, including their investments resulting in at least 10 full-time jobs, they can apply to remove the conditional basis of their green cards. About 10,000 EB–5 visas are made available to qualified applicants each fiscal year.

My remarks today summarize a report GAO issued last fall to this committee providing information on proposed EB–5 investments in TEAs. For that report, we selected and reviewed a random sample of 200 of the approximately 6,600 investor petitions submitted during the fourth quarter of fiscal year 2015.

Based on our review of those petitions, we provided information on the proportion of petitioners that did or did not elect to invest in TEA, the proportion of petitioners basing a high-employment TEA on various types of geographic areas, and EB–5 investment as a proportion of the total investment in projects.

With regard to the first area, we estimated that 99 percent of the EB–5 petitioners who filed a petition in the fourth quarter of fiscal year 2015 elected to invest in a project located in a TEA, most within a high-unemployment TEA that is qualifying for a reduced investment threshold of $500,000.

In particular, just under 97 percent elected to invest in a high-unemployment TEA and just under 3 percent in a rural TEA. The remaining petitioners elected to invest at least $1 million in a project that was not located in a TEA.

Second, we estimated that 90 percent of petitioners electing to invest in a high-unemployment TEA based that on the average unemployment rate for a combination of census areas while the remaining 10 percent based the TEA on the employment rate of a single census tract, block group, or a county. Most of these petitioners combined from 2 to 10 census areas, but others combined more than 100 census areas, as allowed under the program as currently structured.

With regard to the third area, we estimated that EB–5 investment by one or more immigrant investors who invested in projects located in a TEA was generally less than the nonEB–5 investment by other U.S. or foreign investors relative to the total estimated project cost. We also estimated that nearly three-fourths of petitioners who elected to invest in a TEA invested or plan to invest in various types of real estate projects, such as hotels and resorts, commercial and residential developments.

In closing, in addition to our September 2016 report regarding proposed investments in TEAs, we have also issued reports related to USCIS' efforts to assess and address fraud within the EB–5 program and to report the economic benefits of the program. We have made recommendations in these areas, which USCIS is working to address, and we will continue to monitor USCIS' efforts and progress.

This concludes my oral statement, and I would be pleased to answer questions members may have.

[Ms. Gambler's written statement is available at the Committee or on the committee repository at: *http://docs.house.gov/meetings/ JU/JU00/20170308/105660/HHRG-11-JU00-Wstate-GambLerR-20170308.pdf*]

Chairman GOODLATTE. Thank you, Ms. Gambler.

Mr. Walls, welcome.

TESTIMONY OF SAM WALLS III

Mr. WALLS. Thank you, Chairman.

Chairman Goodlatte, Ranking Member Conyers, and members of the committee, thank you for the opportunity today to appear today to discuss the EB–5 foreign investor program.

My name is Sam Walls, and I am the president and chief operating officer of Arkansas Capital Corporation. Arkansas Capital Corporation is a private, nonprofit, economic development company that was formed in 1957 by State business leaders that included the late Governor Winthrop Rockefeller. We partner with banks and other sources to provide capital to businesses starting or expanding in our State.

In 2012, State leadership requested Arkansas Capital to create an EB–5 regional center that would serve Arkansas. This request was made of Arkansas Capital because of our impeccable reputation and history of partnering with the State to promote economic development. Pine State Regional Center was approved in 2014.

In September of 2015, Pine State filed its first EB–5 exemplar petition to raise up to $200 million for a $1.67 billion steel manufacturer in Osceola, Arkansas, a rural community with high unemployment, persistent high poverty levels, and a low level of college degrees. State and local leaders have described this steel production facility as a game changer and a godsend. This facility is the largest industrial project in the history of the State of Arkansas. The project creates 9,600 construction direct and indirect jobs. The employees of this facility will earn wages with benefits that far exceed the average salary in that community and what most would ever have dreamt possible.

But to be clear, although we are proud of our involvement in this project, our support for the reforms in the USCIS proposed regulations and in past legislative efforts are not merely because they may provide some benefit to our current project. As a now 60-year-old economic development entity serving Arkansas, we see these reforms as an opportunity for rural and distressed urban communities to realistically use this program to assist in economic development. Our current project is an example of how rural communities will utilize this program if given the opportunity.

Before I make some remarks about the USCIS proposed EB–5 regulations, I wanted to express my thanks to you, Mr. Chairman, Ranking Member Conyers, Senator Grassley, and Senator Leahy, for your efforts to enact EB–5 reform legislation. We strongly support your legislation introduced in the last Congress and encourage you to continue to push your EB–5 reforms that will help rural and underserved communities.

I applaud USCIS for its proposed regulations on EB–5. Today, the adjective "controversial" almost invariably seems to be used when this program is discussed in public forums. The USCIS is clearly attempting to take whatever steps it can within its authority to reform the program and address these concerns. While we share the view of many in the industry about the rates of increase to the current investment levels, we still welcome the proposed rules for several reasons.

The rules' reform of the targeted employment area destination would return the use of this designation to the original intent of Congress. Currently, some of the most affluent areas of the country have been able to attain the TEA designation by creatively streaming together dozens of disparate census tracts. The TEA designation was intended for rural and highly distressed urban areas and was anticipated to be exception, not the rule. According to the Government Accountability Office, we know that, today, more than 90 percent of investors have gone into projects that are in urban TEAs comprised of many, sometimes dozens, of census tracts, and only 3 percent of EB–5 investments have gone into rural areas.

We agree with the chairman in his observation that this practice has made a mockery of what Congress intended.

The proposed regulations essentially maintain the current statutory differential between the TEA and non-TEA investment levels of 500,000. From our perspective, this is a key component to the TEA reform because a more restrictive process to qualify for TEA status is only half of the equation. There must be a meaningful difference in the investment amounts. Past suggestions of a $50,000 difference, for example, will amount to a continuation of the status quo. The program's legislative history is clear on this point: the discounted investment rate was intended to drive investment to areas of the country that are traditionally undercapitalized. A meaningful investment differential is essential to achieve that goal.

The proposed rule is important for another reason. Over the past 2 years, we have seen a small segment of the EB–5 industry essentially veto proposed reforms. Most recently, this past December, these stakeholders rejected a very fair reform compromise. Like any compromise, they were asked to accept things that we didn't like, but taken as a whole, it was fair, and we support it with an eye toward the long-term health and viability of the program.

If finalized, these proposed regulations will finally make this on-going strategy of delay untenable for these parties and force them to participate in good faith in the legislative process.

All of you have heard arguments against making changes to the EB–5 program. Some have claimed that proposed legislative reforms are picking winners and losers. We believe that efforts to restore congressional intent to the EB–5 TEA incentive is not picking winners and losers. It is an effort to fix a broken program.

Some claim that the EB–5 program is just a job creation program, and so it should not matter where investments are going as long as jobs are being created somewhere. Some argue that the TEA policy is being honored if people commute from poor areas to prospering areas where an EB–5 project is. This argument completely ignores the fact that Congress enacted the TEA incentive for a very specific purpose: to boost economic activity in communities that are traditionally undercapitalized. Congress would not have debated and enacted the TEA provision on the assumption it would apply everywhere. Congress has every right to insist that public policy work as it was intended.

If the recent Presidential election showed us anything, it demonstrated that there are numerous rural and distressed urban communities that feel the government has forgotten about them. The clear intent of the TEA designation was an effort by Congress to help induce more job-creating economic investment in those areas, a result that has not been realized yet.

The reforms contained in the USCIS proposed regulations and recent legislative efforts is a reaffirmation to the people in those areas of the country that Congress has not forgotten about them and is working to help those communities restore vital sources of employment.

Thank you, and I look forward to your questions.

[Mr. Walls' written statement is available at the Committee or on the committee repository at: *http://docs.house.gov/meetings/ JU/JU00/20170308/105660/HHRG-115-JU00-Wstate-WallsS- 20170308.pdf*]

Chairman GOODLATTE. Thank you, Mr. Walls.

Ms. Brunner, welcome.

TESTIMONY OF ANGELIQUE BRUNNER

Ms. BRUNNER. Chairman Goodlatte, Ranking Member Conyers, and distinguished members of the committee, thank you for the opportunity to testify today.

My name is Angelique Brunner, and I am founder and president of EB5 Capital, a regional center operator based in Maryland. I founded the company in 2007 in the District of Columbia to utilize foreign capital in disadvantaged communities and support living-wage job creation. Founding the company during the economic downturn gave me a unique perspective on capital markets, their lack of resilience, and the importance of a flexible, independent source of capital.

Today, EB5 Capital is a leading regional center operator. We manage more than $400 million of investment capital that represents more than 20 projects in five States and the District of Columbia on behalf of clients from 50 countries.

Our investments have anchored more than $2.4 billion of total development that has created thousands of jobs. The company's initial focus was Washington, D.C., where we have committed over $250 million of investment in transitioning communities in the Convention Center corridor, the ballpark and Capitol Riverfront area, and most recently in NOMA, where Uline Arena is reshaping the entire neighborhood with REI's flagship store and the District's first creative class A offices.

Our expansion outside of the District includes projects throughout California and the entire State of Michigan, where we believe that we can bring $100 million a year for qualified EB–5 projects under the current TEA definitions.

I am here today to comment on proposed regulations that, if enacted, will jeopardize the ability of the program to continue to draw foreign direct investment to the United States. I urge Congress to complete the legislative reform of the EB–5 program that your committee has been working on with stakeholders for the past 2 years. Regulatory changes in support of new legislation could then be revisited after congressional action.

The most problematic proposed changes that I will focus on are the changes to the targeted employment area definition and the increases in investment amounts. On their face, both may seem grounded in principled arguments, but with further examination, the economic basis of both are subjective and far from a best-practices approach to the reform each is meant to foster.

My first area of concern is that the proposed TEA definition does not incorporate preexisting government criteria. DHS is proposing to continue the single variable criteria of a targeted employment area. I was hopeful that DHS would propose new criteria practiced elsewhere in Federal Government, like those used to define the new market tax credit qualifying geography, or eliminate the TEA entirely.

Additionally, proposed limitations based on number of census tracts are biased against densely populated urban areas that have significantly more census tracts per square mile than suburban and rural areas. The suggested doughnut approach that measures economic development as a circle of adjacent census tracts rather than commuting distance does not reflect the reality of economic development in cities which follow a block-by-block path and/or occur along public transit lines. To illustrate this bias, I offer an anecdote from my commute to the hearing from my office this morning, an 8.3-mile drive. If I take a suburban route, I travel only 10 census tracts. But if I travel through the District of Columbia, I cover 21 census tracts.

My second area of concern is that the market will not support the proposed increase in investment levels. At this time, the EB–5 program is effectively operated as a one-tier level of investment, with 95 percent of investments occurring at the $500,000 level, which DHS proposes raising to $1.35 million. Such an increase will shock the marketplace and, in my opinion, decimate the EB–5 program.

U.S. competes for investors with about 40 countries. Our ability to attract investors is already compromised because of our complex immigration requirements, visa capacity issues, and processing backlogs. An increase in investment amount at the magnitude proposed.

While the investment tiers of $501 million date back to the beginning of the program, the higher investment amount has never been competitive.

Success and reform can be aligned. Incentives for rural and distressed urban areas through visa set-asides will achieve the investments expressed by many stakeholders. Reform efforts should shift away from the arbitrary single variable TEA to a single investment amount. Given the program's backlog, investors want their visas quicker. A single investment amount, eliminating the TEA, coupled with set-asides will incent increased investment in needed areas.

In conclusion, Mr. Chairman, Ranking Member Conyers, and distinguished members of the committee, I strongly urge you to advise the current administration to cancel the regulations proposed by the previous administration. I ask that you instead support Congress to complete its work on legislative reform of the EB–5 program. Regulatory changes in support of new legislation could then be revisited after congressional action.

Thank you. This concludes my statement, and I would be pleased to answer questions.

[Ms. Brunner's written statement is available at the Committee or on the committee repository at: *http://docs.house.gov/meetings/ JU/JU00/20170308/105660/HHRG-115-JU00-Wstate-BrunnerA-20170308.pdf*]

Chairman GOODLATTE. Thank you, Ms. Brunner.

Ms. Mends-Cole, welcome.

TESTIMONY OF DEKONTI MENDS-COLE

Ms. MENDS-COLE. Thank you, Chairman Goodlatte, Ranking Member Conyers, and distinguished members of the committee. Thank you for inviting me to testify today. As stated, my name is Dekonti Mends-Cole and I serve as the director of policy for Center for Community Progress based in Washington, D.C.

The Center for Community Progress is a national nonprofit focused on addressing vacancy and abandonment to revitalize distressed communities in urban, suburban, and rural areas. Headquartered in Flint, Michigan, with staff in Detroit, upstate New York, New Orleans, Chicago, and Atlanta, our organization supports the revitalization of America's older industrial regions and places, as well as communities that for decades have experienced an exodus of population and industry. We believe that a reformed EB–5 program that presents an opportunity to revitalize places experiencing economic distress and in the greatest need of at-risk capital to spur growth, such as Detroit, Michigan; Cincinnati, Ohio; and Scranton, Pennsylvania, would provide the greatest benefit.

The EB–5 program introduced in 1990 was intended to be an innovative financing tool that encouraged job growth, incentivized investment, and recruited at-risk capital to disinvested communities.

The program was largely dormant until the 2010s when increased immigrant interests, largely from China, coupled with increased demand for low cost mezzanine finance drove take-up.

At the same time EB–5's use began to increase exponentially, a widening disparity began to emerge between recovering markets and those that are currently on a downward trajectory. From 2010 to 2013, the most prosperous 10 percent of ZIP Codes saw unemployment climb by 22 percent, and the number of businesses rise by 11 percent, while the most distressed 10 percent of ZIP Codes lost 13 percent of their jobs and saw a business closure rate of 1 in 10. Fifty million Americans live in the country's most distressed communities, characterized by low job growth, high vacancy, and out of work adults as high as 55 percent.

The program has become disconnected from its original purpose. Immigrant investor capital, rather than serving as a catalyst for growth in communities serving job and industry loss, has sought the safe havens of high-return and low-risk projects in the country's most prosperous census tracts. This has been made possible by the gerrymandering of EB–5 investment areas. It is not a coincidence that EB–5 capital is heavily concentrated in the States and ZIP Codes with the highest populations living in prosperous census tracts: California, New York, Texas, New Jersey, and Illinois. I hope to shift the EB–5 conversation beyond high density, high growth, largely coastal cities, and support the Department of Homeland Security's efforts to better target EB–5 capital and stimulate economic growth in America's distressed communities.

I would like to specifically talk about the narrowing definition of TEAs that was focused on in the proposed regulations. A February 2017 article by EB–5 experts and scholars, Professor Friedland and Calderon at Stern's business school, applied the following proposed regulation TEA definitions to a sample of 52 projects that were largely from what is known as gateway cities. Based on this application, 52 of the sample qualified projects, only two would apply under a single census tract and only four would qualify under the contiguous census tract definition. This demonstrates that a narrower TEA definition would prohibit projects from continuing to include high unemployment areas that are in close proximity but are not receiving any direct investment from the project. It also would better align with similarly targeted programs such as new market tax credits.

The proposed regulations would more effectively target credits to hard to recruit capital areas than also two other models that have been proposed: The California 12-tract model or the commuting pattern model. Both of these models will continue to permit investors to enter at a lowered investment level and high growth census tracts. It's applied nationally and are less likely to recruit capital for distressed communities than what is outlined in the proposed regulation.

Lastly, I'd like to briefly comment on the deferential between TEAs and non-TEAs. The current legislation has proven to be a valuable incentive for both investors and regional centers. EB–5 investment is completely at risk and investors seeking to minimize their risk have favored lower cost of entry projects in TEA designated areas. A sizable differential is necessary to attract capital to the most economically distressed areas. Ensuring that the spread is continued and adequately incentivizes immigrant investors to support difficult-to-finance projects is necessary.

Thank you for the opportunity to present, and I would be happy to take any questions.

[Ms. Mends-Cole's written statement is available at the Committee or on the committee repository at: *http://docs.house.gov/meetings/JU/JU00/20170308/105660/HHRG-115-JU00-Wstate-Mends-ColeD-20170308.pdf*]

Chairman GOODLATTE. Thank you, Ms. Mends-Cole.

Mr. North, welcome.

TESTIMONY OF DAVID NORTH

Mr. NORTH. Good morning, Mr. Chairman, Mr. Ranking Member, members. I'm grateful for a chance to discuss the proposed changes in the regs of the EB–5 program. I speak for the Center for Immigration Studies. It is a downtown agency, nonpartisan research organization here in Washington, D.C.

Frankly, we have no need for an immigrant investor program. EB–5 brings in only 1 or 2 percent of the flood of new foreign money that is invested in the United States every year, and it brings it in through a convoluted way that almost invites corruption and theft. It is lodged in an agency that does not deal in high finance, involves the sale of visas to aliens who could not become U.S. immigrants in any other way. The Center has moral objections to selling green cards.

That said, realistically, the chances are that the big urban monied interests that profit from the EB–5 program, heavily in Manhattan I might add, it never places—the program never places investments in the Appalachias—will prevail. The big money people will as they usually do. But if the termination battle is lost, perhaps we can make some modest and sensible changes in the program. I have four specific suggestions, two echoing what the Department suggests, and two that don't appear to be in the Department's proposals.

As far as the basic investment is concerned, moving it up to $1.35 million makes a lot of sense to me. Bring in more money without spending more visas in the process. I also disagree with one of my colleagues here at this table about the prospective market. There is a whole lot of fear among a whole lot of very rich people, primarily in China, and I think that the market for visas at $1.35 million will be quite brisk. Besides, we have a backlog to take care of anyway.

The question of the location of the investments is interesting. This is a TEA. Currently, the half million dollar investments must be used in what the agency calls targeted employment areas. I would like to illustrate how this definition can be manipulated in terms of this place. We are in Rayburn House Office Building and the Rayburn House Office Building, as you can see on the screen, is in that kind of upside down U shape form, the red form there. That is a TEA that could be created—I am not saying it has been—it could be created under the current rules, and includes the White House, which is one of the more expensive residences in the country, and this wonderful building. And it is a depressed area as far as DHS is concerned. If you can put the White House in a TEA, you can put a TEA anywhere in the country.

I want to stress something that I am not sure is in the regulation package, and that is the question of integrity. There are numerous, multimillion dollar scandals in this program, in South Dakota, in Vermont, in Chicago, in Florida, in the State of Washington, and lots and lots of them in California. There needs to be a different focus in the administration on these things. And let me give you one example of a particular fraud.

I decided to see—this is regarding one of the California frauds—what I could find out about the proposers of what turns out to be fraudulent activity by using the internet. I am not skilled with the internet. I had no particular law enforcement connections. I just went on the internet and I looked. And what did I find? Well, the first thing I found, that the main broker was a lawyer who had been to a for-profit law school, which is worrisome to me. He had a debt counseling firm attached to his law firm. That sounds worrying. He had been twice sanctioned by the California bar, and when once was suspended from the practice of law for 7 months.

Now, do you want to invest in a program that is led by somebody like that? I would think not. But none of the 100 or so investors did what I had just done in a few minutes, nor had the managers of the EB–5 program. There needs to be a rather more careful approach to who gets to run these programs and who the middlemen are.

There is one other thing that I didn't see in the regs, which I think should be there, and that should be a provision that there be jobs for residents only. There was a failed project in South Dakota where Korean workers were brought in, I think H–2Bs, to build a beef slaughterhouse, and there were Germans working on tourist visas on a German-connected EB–5 lumber mill in Florida. Now, these matters are deplorable, and I think that if any jobs were to be created by this program, they should go to full-time legal residents of this country, including green card holders.

In closing, I would like to point out an irony. This is a program which has been defended stoutly by the leadership, the Republican leadership of the House and the Senate through the continuing resolution that Mr. Sensenbrenner talked about. They have done so despite the fact that two-thirds of the money in this program goes into States that supported Ms. Clinton in the last election. So it may be an act of generosity on the part of the Republican Party to continue a program that is so nice to the blue States.

And on that note, I end.

[Mr. North's written statement is available at the Committee or on the committee repository at: *http://docs.house.gov/meetings/JU/JU00/20170308/105660/HHRG-115-JU00-Wstate-NorthD-20170308.pdf*]

Chairman GOODLATTE. Thank you, Mr. North.

We will now begin questioning by the members of the committee. And I will recognize myself for 5 minutes.

Ms. Gambler, let me start with you. I find it interesting that the General Accounting Office found that three-quarters of all alien investors in TEAs invest in real estate projects, and yet real estate construction accounts for about 6 percent of the U.S. economy. So why does 75 percent of these investments go into what is only 6 percent of the economy?

Ms. GAMBLER. Congressman, that is not something we looked at specifically as part of our review. It may be due to the universe of projects that are available for investors to seek to invest in. So it could be a product of just the types of projects that are available to investors and that that is more predominantly in certain industries than others.

Chairman GOODLATTE. Is it possible that under the current law and regulation, where gerrymandering can allow you to figure development in highly attractive areas like the Hudson Yards example that we used earlier, that the money would gravitate toward what would be considered to be easier investments than it would be to invest the money in a rural area or in a high unemployment area?

Ms. GAMBLER. I think it is reasonable that the types of projects that are available for investors to invest in are probably driven by a number of factors, including what is currently allowed under law and regulation in terms of how projects and regional centers can designate TEAs or can have—use TEAs that have been designated.

Chairman GOODLATTE. Thank you.

Mr. Walls, I read your testimony. It is easy to imagine that projects such as the Big River Steel in Osceola, Arkansas, are the exact type of projects that Congress wanted to facilitate in creating the investor visa program and the regional center program. Isn't it disappointing that so few such projects get funded through this program?

Mr. WALLS. It is. I think, you know, when we were asked to do this and you got into the program without any previous experience, you look at the regs and you say, well, there is TEAs and there is non-TEAs. Clearly, a project like that would fall onto a TEA. And intuitively you would say, well, this clearly looks like a good job creator. And so when you get more immersed into it and you discover that you are competing with very impressive projects in very affluent areas of the country, it is—it is disappointing, it is frustrating, it has been.

Chairman GOODLATTE. And it is highlighted by the fact that, well, this would be considered a less attractive area for the most part for investments, Big River Steel is going to pay its mostly non-college educated workers in rural Arkansas $75,000 a year or more. How do you think this compares with the wages that noncollege educated workers will make at the high end hotels and condos that are being built with EB–5 funds?

Mr. WALLS. I would hesitate to speculate to an exact number, but I would assume that it would be much higher.

Chairman GOODLATTE. Ms. Brunner, you state in your testimony that the administration should cancel the proposed regulations and allow Congress to complete the legislative reform of the EB–5 program that your committee has been working on with stakeholders for the past 2 years. Now you mention your involvement with a number of industry groups who, in my experience, have been incredibly resistant to any real reforms and who have, in fact, stymied reform over the past 2 years. These groups like the investor visa program the way it is. They want the investment level to remain low and they want to be able to qualify luxury condo projects as being in depressed areas. If the regulations are canceled, why would they have any more incentive to engage in substantive negotiations than they have over the last 2 years?

Ms. BRUNNER. Mr. Chair, one thing that has happened in the past year is I have become the membership chair and spokesperson for the EB–5 Investment Coalition. Since that time, the statements in my testimony actually reflect the alignment of those groups and that we are prepared to eliminate the TEA, go to a single investment model. And my understanding is that we are very excited to cooperate with your committee and the Senate committee and achieve reform this calendar year.

Chairman GOODLATTE. Well, good. I am definitely glad to hear that.

One of your statements caught my ear, and did Mr. North as well, and that is that current markets will not support the investment amounts that are provided for in these regulations. And yet for a program that for most of its existence never hit the 10,000 green card cap until just 3 years ago when it suddenly mushroomed into not just hitting the cap, but now having a 7- or 8-year waiting list, meaning that there is a backlog of 70,000 to 80,000 green cards that are committed for and in demand right now, this disturbs me for a couple of reasons.

First of all, I think, like Mr. Sensenbrenner, it makes it very clear that this program can justify much higher payments for green cards than investments for green cards, if you will, than is currently provided for. But secondly, it bothers me that this program has been sold like that to people primarily in China, who I don't think have a clue that this program isn't even authorized beyond April of this year. There is no authorization whatsoever for any green card beyond the expiration of the current continuing resolution in April. And yet this industry, if you will, is busy selling green cards in China to people who, you know, I don't think even have any idea that if the program were allowed to expire in April, would have nothing except for a 70,000 to 80,000 green card backlog.

What would happen if that were to occur? And how—what can you tell me about how the people who promote this program in places like China make full disclosure to these people who are making these investments?

Ms. BRUNNER. I can tell you how my company makes full disclosure. We make sure that all of our investors are aware of the pending expiration or the pending reform of the program, is what we are hopeful for.

Chairman GOODLATTE. But you still think it is appropriate to have them go ahead and make investments without the knowledge that the program is even going to continue?

Ms. BRUNNER. No, they do not make investments without that knowledge. That is not a true statement for our investors. They are all aware of the April 28 deadline for Congress and for the industry. And the market has slowed significantly. It slowed because of the expiration and it slowed because of the significant backlog.

I would like to address one of your earlier comments in your statement about the increase demand that we have seen recently.

So we are all well aware here that demand really started in 2008. I would argue that that is when the price matched the demand, which allowed the supply of the visas to be utilized. So it wasn't until 2008 that $500,000 was actually the right price for the market demand.

Now, it seems that $500,000 is a bit low for the market demand, and that it would be better served with an increase in the price. We support that. I support that as a company and as a stakeholder in the industry. What I support, though, is a single investment amount that would drive more investment to distressed areas in a set-aside program instead of forcing them into a reduced investment amount below what the higher qualified areas could receive.

Chairman GOODLATTE. I am way over my time here. I just want to make one more point. I agree with your assessment that a lot of this got started following the financial crisis in 2008, because there was a severe shortage of capital at the time and this became attractive, but it didn't shoot through the roof until you get to about 2013 or 2014. That is the first time we ever hit the cap. And now, in the 3 years since then, when capital has been far more abundant and it has been noted far more capital flows into the United States for other reasons than this reason that we have this huge backlog, and now as we are trying to reform this program, we see tremendous resistance from people who don't want to see greater investments or who don't want to see the reforms take place until this entire investment backlog now 7 or 8 years is worked down. I find that intolerable given the problems the program has.

I am now happy to yield to the gentleman from Michigan, Mr. Conyers, and I will be generous with his time as well.

Mr. CONYERS. Thank you, Mr. Chairman.

Let me start with Ms. Mends-Cole. In your testimony, you mention that your organization works in areas experiencing economic distress. What kinds of EB–5 finance projects can be made in this area, in your view?

Ms. MENDS-COLE. There is a lot of opportunity for EB–5. And examples of existing projects that are on the pipeline are the Hardesty Federal Complex in Kansas City. It is an 18-acre brownfield site in which a nonprofit regional center is looking to secure capital. It is working with Northwest Missouri State University. And the purpose of this project is both the educational facility as well as addressing the needs of a food desert.

Another example is the George Washington bus station restoration which is in a distressed census tract in upper Manhattan. This is a 15,000 square feet development and it is projected to create 250 jobs and has leveraged $5 million worth of tax credits.

Mr. CONYERS. Now, let me follow up on the idea, what kind of revitalizing impact could these projects have on distressed urban areas?

Ms. MENDS-COLE. Both examples in Hardesty Federal Complex and also in your home city of Detroit, Michigan, where Bedrock Ventures is looking at investing utilizing EB–5, specifically looks at vacant properties. Properties—for example, the Hardesty Federal Complex has been abandoned since 2002, and Bedrock's looking at some of the most distressed census tracts in neighborhoods in terms of the abandonment and vacancy in the country.

Mr. CONYERS. Good.

Let me ask Mr. Sam Walls. We have heard testimony today from others in the EB–5 industry that targeted employment areas should take into account commuter patterns, that is whether those working in projects from distressed areas. What are your thoughts about this kind of an approach?

Mr. WALLS. I disagree. The problem with—I look at congressional intent. And if you look at congressional intent, clearly, it wasn't a function of we want to just create jobs and then people that live in those poor areas can commute to those good jobs in better areas of their cities or from rural communities into larger areas around them. Clearly, the congressional intent was looking for investment within those census tracts.

We are an economic development entity so we have a saying around our shop; it is activity begets activity. And so, clearly, what the intent was to see investments physically—actually end those census tracts and then the subsequent advantages that come with that investment. We do a lot with new market tax credits with one of our other entities. And it is the same thought process: Catalytic investment.

And that is clearly what the TEA intent was. And so to modify that to say TEA now as if they can drive somewhere closely, I think is inconsistent with what the intent was to begin with.

Mr. CONYERS. Thank you.

Ms. Brunner, you raise in your testimony concerns that EB–5 program has to compete with about 40 other countries that also have investor programs, and that raising the U.S. investment threshold to over $1 million could make EB–5 noncompetitive. But that doesn't seem to be the case. For example, the United Kingdom offers temporary visas for investments of $2.5 million in effect. Australia has three programs requiring $5 million, $15 million, and $1.5—these are in Australian dollars—and $1.5 million in Australian dollars.

Is there reason to believe that a U.S. investor program cannot compete with these other programs if the investment threshold is raised beyond $565,000 as you propose in your testimony?

Ms. BRUNNER. The demand for the U.K. program and the Australian program in the markets that the U.S. is competitive in, primarily China, is much less than the demand for the U.S. program. To adjust the amount up, I think the market can accommodate some adjustment, but to approach those levels, I think you have to ask yourself, is this an economic development program or is it something else? If it is going to be an economic development program, then we want to maximize the demand at the right price threshold. That is a delicate—that is a delicate task that I think warrants continued conversation, and it certainly is worthy of our effort. But we have to strike that balance if we want to continue funding.

For example, I funded food deserts; I have put 70,000 square feet of retail back into commission in Washington, D.C. My pipeline includes the Greyhound bus station in Washington, D.C. I hope to put hundreds of millions of dollars into the State of Michigan, and I hope to start with the city of Detroit. All of these things are economic development for me. They won't be possible if we raise the investment amount too high.

Mr. CONYERS. Thank you so much.

Mr. Chairman, I yield back.

Mr. KING [presiding]. The gentleman from Michigan yields back the balance of his time.

I now recognize myself for 5 minutes. And I would turn first to Ms. Brunner. I think I heard Mr. North mention that he expects that the Chinese would come up with 1.35 million in lieu of the half million that we are discussing here. What is your estimation of how that might affect their investment in this country should that number be increased to 1.35?

Ms. BRUNNER. Sure. Well, it is one of the reasons why I advocate for the elimination of TEAs. I do not want the market to have an option of a lower investment amount. I want to eliminate that option.

Mr. KING. And do you think if we raised it, then it would affect the flow of capital coming from China into the United States?

Ms. BRUNNER. I think it will. In any supply and demand model you have three variables: You have the supply, you have the demand, and you have the price. The only thing that we can change is the supply of the visas. I understand that is not really—Congress really isn't inclined to do that, so the thing that we can change is price. There seems to be some agreement on that. So we need to figure out the right price to maintain this as an economic development program.

Mr. KING. In listening to Mr. Conyers, did you reflect that other countries are selling access to a path to citizenship at a much higher price than the United States is?

Ms. BRUNNER. Well, no other country in the world uses it for economic development. We are the only country in the world with a job creation requirement.

Mr. KING. You heard the quotes from Mr. Conyers that it was substantially higher than half a million dollars, I think up to $2.5 million in one case. That is what I reflected.

And so if we repeal EB–5, what does that do to the flow of capital into some of the investments that you are promoting?

Ms. BRUNNER. It will stop it.

Mr. KING. And what would be the next source of capital for those investments?

Ms. BRUNNER. Well, I have been in economic development in Washington, D.C. since 1999, and when I came here, the city was selling houses for $1. And I asked why and they said because of the riots. And I said, what riots? And they said the Martin Luther King riots. So I imagined the development would stop.

Mr. KING. I have a bit of a different estimate, but I appreciate your testimony.

I turn to Ms. Gambler, and I just ask you this, when I think about some countries that are not emerging as our friends, China to a degree, Russia to an increasing degree, especially in the last couple of months, if you were Saudi investors and you wanted to infiltrate people who were sympathetic to the cause of some of the people who flew planes into the building, what method would you use to bring those folks into the United States?

Ms. GAMBLER. Well, sir, I think there are a couple of comments in response to that. We do have some ongoing work right now looking at the vetting and background check process for individuals who are coming to the U.S. on visas. And we would be happy to come up and talk with you about that as well, about what that work is.

With regard to the EB–5 program, we have identified through our work some concerns with fraud in the program. We have talked about that a little bit this morning. And that is why it is important, as it relates this program, for USCIS to do the fraud risk assessments that we have been calling for them to do to include identifying what the inherent risks are in the program.

Mr. KING. Let's just say you are a drug cartel in Mexico and you want to get some of your people into the United States. They are the masters at laundering money. And so to be able to trace that back to them, but the dollars and identify whether or not those people are affiliated, it seems to be to be a very difficult task. Second thing would be, from a national security standpoint, although I always hear vetting, better vetting, extreme vetting. But I am not one who is convinced we can actually vet people when their children become radicalized. And so I will submit that if you are strategizing against the interest of the United States and you want your people into America and you had money and you wanted a return on that investment, you would look at the EB–5 program as the perfect tool for access into the American society and, by the way, to be able to maneuver and operate throughout the business circles in the United States.

I was on a plane not that long ago, a man sat next to me and I ask him what he did. We had that little conversation. He was putting together an EB–5 hotel, a $30 million hotel that had 60 Chinese investors. And I wonder, would that hotel be built if it weren't for EB–5. But I am going to turn to Mr. North with that question, would that hotel be built if it weren't for EB–5?

Mr. NORTH. In many cases, the EB–5 program is an income transfer program from rich Chinese to rich Americans. What happens is there is something called mezzanine financing, which is the financing that goes into real estate developments where you do not have either ownership or a mortgage, and so it is kind of risky. And mezzanine financing typically produces—again I am not an economist, I don't do this sort of thing—but produces a fairly substantial interest rate because there is no guarantees.

However, if you bring in EB–5 money, not looking for guarantees particularly, they can get their mezzanine financing for about 1 percent. So there is—I am sure there are hotels that would not have been—or projects that would not have happened without the EB–5. In most cases, it is just simply a question of making it easier and more profitable for the U.S. developers.

Mr. KING. Does anybody on the panel know how much U.S. capital is stranded overseas because of our current tax policy? That number would be in the trillions. Does anybody have that number?

Mr. NORTH. It is a big number, but it is—I think it is beyond my expertise.

Mr. KING. I would submit that repatriating U.S. capital would be a far better thing to do than to open our doors up for these kind of nefarious activities that appear to me to be taking place.

I thank you, all the witnesses, and I yield back the balance of my time.

I now recognize the gentlelady from California, Ms. Lofgren.

Ms. LOFGREN. Thank you, Mr. Chairman.

I don't know if anyone can answer this question, but this is obviously something that is program of interest both to the Congress but also to the executive branch. In the newspapers it has been reported that a key adviser to President Trump, his son-in-law, Jared Kushner, has used the EB–5 program to build hotels and other investments in New York City. Is that true? And if that is true, I wonder whether we might ask the administration to take steps to guard against being influenced by the financial benefit to that key adviser.

Mr. NORTH. If I may, I sense that the Kushner family has heavily invested with EB–5 money in Jersey City, which is right across the river from midtown Manhattan. I do not know if there are— and the enterprise is a Trump center—Trump Plaza, excuse me— I do not know whether there are any EB–5 projects in New York City that are funded for the Trump family from EB–5. I don't know about that, but there is one right across the River.

Ms. LOFGREN. Does anyone else know about this? Perhaps it is unfair, you wouldn't necessarily know. But I think some research ought to be done on that, Mr. Chairman, to make sure that we are getting unbiased participation by the executive.

Just a word on the investment level. I come from Silicon Valley where recently a double wide was put up—double-wide trailer was put up for sale for almost $400,000. So a $500,000 investment seems incredible. You know, this has got to be updated. In looking at the investments required by other countries, I think a substantial increase is required. I will just put that out there.

One of the questions I have is whether, in addition to looking at the dollar amount, whether we ought to—and the gerrymandering, whether we ought to look at the nature of the investments themselves. You know, recently, somebody who is doing a project said that the funding through EB–5 was being used for the basic infrastructure. Well, you can't get a bank loan to do the sewers and the infrastructure that then allows development on top of that. Would it make sense for us to direct these funds to something that then creates a platform for investment from other sources to be successful? Does anybody have a thought on that?

Apparently not. But at a later date, I mean, I think that that is—we ought to take a look at what promotes development and growth and job structure best. And right now, this is primarily used as funding for hotel construction. I am certainly not against hotel construction if it makes sense, but that is certainly not the only economic need, and some might argue, not the most important economic need in the United States.

You know, I was wondering, Mr. North, you mentioned the reform that was necessary. I am thinking about, if we do a reform package, when that reform should be put into place. There is a backlog I think of nearly—well, it is over 20,000 petitions, and some have argued that the—whatever reform that we do, assuming we get there, should be instituted only after the backlog is cleared. Others have said if you do that, we might as well not do the reform, because there is such a backlog in hand.

I am wondering if anybody has an observation on the timing of reform question.

Mr. NORTH. I do. I think that to postpone it until all the backlog is used is kicking the can down the road squared, and I don't think it should be done that way. There may be a problem about changing the dollar value. I don't think you can change the dollar value of the minimum investment retroactively, but I think you certainly can immediately——

Ms. LOFGREN. Well, I think certainly you can. I don't think the people have a vested actionable interest in a law that could be changed by the Congress.

Mr. NORTH. But I think that the administrative reforms that I have been suggesting and also the TEA reform should be done right away.

Ms. LOFGREN. I know my time is close to running out. Ms. Gambler, you had important testimony last year about the immigrant investors who were vulnerable to fraud schemes. And I am wondering, in addition to all of the investor alerts that were done, what further steps USCIS should take to protect innocent investors from being defrauded.

Ms. GAMBLER. There are a couple of key issues there, Congresswoman. One, as I mentioned, they have made progress on doing fraud risk assessments identified the inherent risks in the program. They need to continue to do that. I think they also need to continue to look at the fraud prevention and assessment tools that they do have, including things like random site visits to some of these projects, doing interviews and proving the data and information they are collecting from investors and regional centers. So they have made some progress in these areas, but there is additional work they could do.

Ms. LOFGREN. Just one final question. It is—some have suggested that the middlemen that are essentially charging very high fees to investors outside the United States for kind of act as the broker have not really been scrutinized adequately by our government. Do you have insight into that allegation?

Ms. GAMBLER. That is part of some of the unique fraud risks that our report from 2015 identified. And we would say that is part of assessing the risk in the program. That could be one of the inherent risks that should be looked at.

Ms. LOFGREN. Okay. My time has expired, Mr. Chairman. Thank you very much.

Mr. KING [presiding]. The gentlelady's time has expired.

The chair now recognizes the gentleman from California, Mr. Issa.

Mr. ISSA. Thank you, Mr. Chairman.

Mr. NORTH. Senator Feinstein has called EB–5 selling citizenship. Some might say renting for citizenship. But is there any reason to say that if this is a good program, we should cap it at 10,000? If we're going to sell citizenship and earn $1.5 billion a year of loaned money for a total of about $7.5 billion in investment, in this $18 trillion, $19 trillion economy, we have 1.2 million people who receive green cards, why not sell them all? Why not make it 100,000 and be getting $15 billion a year if it is a good thing? So the question is are we selling citizenship?

Mr. NORTH. Well, first of all, to be narrow, we are selling green cards rather than citizenship.

Mr. ISSA. Yes. Green cards lead to the ability to have citizenship.

Mr. NORTH. I understand that.

Mr. ISSA. So we are selling the ability to permanently be here. Maybe I will phrase it to you another way. Why is it we see sell for a temporary loan, a temporary investment, a permanent right to be here? Why wouldn't we have temporary visas for temporary investment?

Mr. NORTH. I don't think renting or selling visas is a good idea. I think it is amoral; if not immoral. I would be opposed to it, but— and that is our basic position.

Mr. ISSA. Okay. Well, it is not my basic position, but I could get there if we can't reform it.

Mr. Walls, regional centers by definition, by testimony, essentially get—are part of giving us, whether gerrymandered or not, virtually 100 percent of the investments are made at 500,000 per investor. That is right. So if we assume for a moment under current rules—we will forget about whether they are gerrymandered or not—that all the investment is going to underserved areas, why wouldn't we simply eliminate any investment except in underserved areas? In other words, since desirable areas shouldn't have a problem getting money, and I would say that Beverly Hills is pretty desirable, but assuming that we are only talking undesirable, for such a small program that is so oversubscribed, why wouldn't we go to 1.8 or 2 million per investment and have them only in underserved areas? Why would we have two tiers at all? Why wouldn't we just mandate that the only way you get in and get what Mr. Walls, Mr. North and I might consider to be selling residency, why wouldn't we require that you invest in underserved areas?

Mr. WALLS. Well, I think there are two questions there. One, you know, what is the dollar amount? And I actually agree with the industry and Ms. Brunner that, you know, I think there needs to be additional conversation as to what the true market for what we should charge, though. So setting that aside.

Mr. Issa. But you know the true market is a lot higher than what we are currently charging?

Mr. WALLS. Absolutely.

Mr. ISSA. The oversubscription tells us that.

Mr. WALLS. We agree to that. We agree. It is just what that number is.

As far as—again, you go to congressional, what do you want this program to do? Clearly, it appears to me that the intent was to— you know, this two tiered of, hey, if it is a good project and creates jobs regardless where it is, we are prepared to accept that, but, you know, there is less risk there, real or perceived. And we as a country are prepared to put a certain amount, a dollar amount. But if you want to—we want to encourage economic development in these areas, we will give it a break and try to mitigate that risk.

Mr. ISSA. What is interesting is I have looked at the history of it, and, of course, two things that were assumed: One is that the investors and the entrepreneurs would come together, that somehow there would be a connection. But in fact, in almost every case, the investor—the green card holder goes one place and the money goes another, and there is no participation almost always. So we failed in that presumption.

We also set aside about 3,000 of 10,000 slots for underserved. That was to assume that it would still be hard to get them into underserved.

Mr. WALLS. Right.

Mr. ISSA. So if eventually we live up to what Senator Grassley and the chairman had been working on so long and hard with members on the other side also, maybe what we need is a set-aside without a discount, because ultimately, then you would get that amount in underserved areas and you could be stringent about it, but you wouldn't necessarily be selling anything for less, because right now, the incentive has been get to the lower price. But the incentive does not seem to be get to the true underserved area.

Ms. Brunner, you are shaking your head in a way that I really want to know your answer.

Ms. BRUNNER. Well, thank you, Congressman. I am extremely in favor of a single price because I don't think that it is fair that if you are designated a set-aside area, distressed area, or rural area, that means then that you have to compromise and receive less capital.

Mr. ISSA. The——

Mr. WALLS. If I may answer the question as well.

Mr. Issa. Go ahead.

Mr. WALLS. I just—respectfully, if you are going to drive—again, the intent behind it was those underserved areas have challenges. Congress deals with those challenges in a number—new market tax credits; USDA guarantees; in my area, Delta Regional Authority. Saying there is one tier, and the set---aside is a short-term answer to that, but involvement in the market, without a true meaningful difference in that, you are not going to ultimately accomplish what you say——

Mr. ISSA. Let me just ask a closing question for the entire panel, with your indulgence, Chairman. Is it fair to say that if we were doing an overall today, and if we set the price where we knew 10,000 slots, and all 10,000 would be sold, whatever that price is, is if fair to say that we look at original intent and the best and the highest use for this investment, that really all of it should go to underserved areas? Whatever that definition is. We don't think it is Manhattan or Beverly Hills, but just a general yes, would you say if we were starting over from scratch and assuming we are not killing the program, we are setting at a price at some level, and because so many agree to a single rate, isn't the best part of what this program could do is get investment where it otherwise wouldn't go, which is underserved areas? Please, if I could get a yes or no from each of you.

Mr. NORTH. I would say yes. Yes.

Ms. MENDS-COLE. I would also say yes.

Ms. BRUNNER. I would say yes, but the goal is to create the highest wage living—living wage jobs.

Mr. ISSA. Good point.

Mr. WALLS. Yes.

Ms. GAMBLER. Yes.

Mr. ISSA. Thank you. I will quit on yes.

Mr. KING. The gentleman's time has expired.

And the chair now recognizes the gentlelady from Texas, Ms. Jackson Lee.

Ms. JACKSON LEE. First, I would like to thank the witnesses for I think a very thoughtful discussion. And I believe that there is value to the EB–5, but let me be very clear. As we have listened to some of the reforms, I just wonder why we sell ourselves so cheap, putting aside present governmental challenges. This is a great country to come to, a great country to invest in. And from recent international trips, one that many people are eager to come to.

So let me ask Ms. Brunner the first question. And let me thank you for your work and Ms. Mends-Cole's work. What is the amount that you would think would be viable? And you are supporting the one tier as opposed to—and that would be how much?

Ms. BRUNNER. I am going to have to lean heavily on my Princeton economics background on this.

Mr. ISSA. Go Tigers.

Ms. BRUNNER. Go Tigers.

I would have to say that that can be modeled, and I would look to the GAO's work and I would look to the committee's work that we should be able to actually mathematically find that price. And that is the price that I would support. I agree that it is above $500,000. I believe, from my experience in the market, with almost a 1,000 investors, that that amount is less than $1 million.

Ms. JACKSON LEE. So I would probably—and I appreciate both the cautiousness, but also the intellectual assessment which is that you look at the economic modeling. But I would immediately go to $1 million to $2 million. And I think we are, in essence, undermining the competition here in the United States. We are undermining the viability of projects, if we would be at that level. I don't even know we can do it with $500,000. I guess it is used as a leverage, or $750,000.

So I would argue against modeling—well, I wouldn't argue against modeling, but I would argue against anything below $1 million, and I would argue for $2 million. But I think the EB–5 program has a great deal of merit, but let me ask—and so thank you.

Let me ask Ms. Gambler, if I could, to indicate in your review, in your reform—or in your suggested reform or reforms, does the regional centers go away?

Ms. GAMBLER. So it is not our proposed reform——

Ms. JACKSON LEE. DHS.

Ms. GAMBLER. I am with GAO. I am so sorry.

Ms. JACKSON LEE. I understand. Does DHS go away? Does the regional centers go away?

Ms. GAMBLER. Under DHS's current proposals and the regulation, no, there is no proposal to eliminate the regional centers.

Ms. JACKSON LEE. And what is your assessment of the regional centers?

Ms. GAMBLER. Based on the work that we have done, I think there are some questions about them, particularly as it relates to EB–5 investors being able to take credit for all of the jobs created by the total investment in projects that are funded through regional centers and other projects as well. So I think there are some open questions that stakeholders and Congress has raised about the program.

Ms. JACKSON LEE. And do see the reforms helping with the gerrymandering aspect so that you don't draw in Beverly Hills along with maybe one or two blocks that are distressed?

Ms. GAMBLER. The proposed rulemaking on the TEA seems to be a reasonable step forward to addressing some of the concerns that have been raised by the TEAs. And I think USCIS seeking comments from the public and from stakeholders and industry will be helpful to inform that rulemaking process as well, including asking for feedback and input on the potential effects of changes to the TEAs.

Ms. JACKSON LEE. And let me give three questions and then you all can answer them. To you, Ms. Gambler, what about the ability of the Immigration Services to vet the whole project and economic aspect of it; in your review, what did you see in that?

Let me ask questions to Mr. Walls. How do you respond to arguments that the current system operates as a one-tier level investment?

And then to Ms. Mends-Cole, the cited projects that you had in distressed areas, if these projects are already happening, why do you think the program needs reform?

So, Ms. Gambler, on the review by the Immigration Services, do they have the wherewithal to do so? Should we set up a certain—another entity to do that?

Ms. GAMBLER. So I don't know for certain that they would have the staff with the right skills and abilities. But what I would say is, in the past, both we and the DHS IG have reported in other areas related to the EB–5 program on the need for USCIS to increase staff in both numbers and skills. And USCIS has been taking steps to do that over the course of the past few years.

Ms. JACKSON LEE. Mr. Walls.

Mr. WALLS. I agree that it has been operating as a one-tier investment system, but it was contrary to the intent of congressional intent. It was intended to be a two tier. It just has operated a one tier because of misuse of the TEA designation.

Ms. JACKSON LEE. And Ms. Mends-Cole.

Ms. MENDS-COLE. These projects have largely been happening not because of but despite of the current status quo. I believe that a reform would allow for greater geographic distribution both at a national level, but also within a State level. So some of the projects that were discussed are largely heavily in New York, upstate New York. Places like Utica that desperately need these dollars have been overlooked because of the attraction for at-risk capital to very low risk investments.

Ms. JACKSON LEE. Thank you.

Mr. Chairman, I would just like to conclude by saying I think it is very important that this committee looks to improving distressed areas and creating jobs in all areas, both urban and rural, and I hope we can do this together. With that, I yield back.

Mr. KING. The chair thanks the gentlelady from Texas.

And now recognizes the gentleman from Idaho, Mr. Labrador.

Mr. LABRADOR. Thank you, Mr. Chairman. And thank you to all the witnesses for being here today.

As you know, Senator Grassley testified that the original intent of the investor visa program was to create new employment for American workers and infuse capital into distressed or rural areas.

Ms. Gambler, is the program accomplishing those goals?

Ms. GAMBLER. Based on the sample of files that we looked at for the report we issued to this committee last year, we found that the majority of projects within our sample were going to areas or were located in census tracts, census areas that had unemployment rates of 6 percent or less. So the majority of projects in the sample we looked at, they were located in areas that had an unemployment rate of 6 percent or less.

Mr. LABRADOR. Okay. Mr. Walls, in the past I have expressed concerns about how gerrymandered districts have led to so many urban projects in low unemployment areas, while the rural communities and the true high end unemployment urban centers have been largely forgotten. Do you think the proposed regulatory changes stopped the gerrymandering that has been occurring?

Mr. WALLS. Yes. Sorry, the microphone comes in and out.

Mr. LABRADOR. That is okay.

Mr. WALLS. Yes. As proposed, it does address the gerrymandering issue.

Mr. LABRADOR. Okay. Mr. North, same question. Are the proposed changes to the TEA definition sufficient to end the gerrymandering that has been occurring in the program?

Mr. NORTH. I think it helps. I would rather do it the way the—some of you may recall in this room—the Appalachian regional development commission was done. You would have to put your investment in a previously defined depressed county, which was the minority of the United States, the minority of the geography of the United States. If you do it that way, then Congress has some control over it. Otherwise, various creative people do as they are currently doing, and I don't like that.

Mr. LABRADOR. Okay. Mr. Walls, my State Idaho like Arkansas is a rural State and I am concerned about the lack of investment going to those areas. Will the proposed changes lead to more investment in those areas?

Mr. WALLS. Well, I think, again, our motivation is the changes are a step towards that. We agree with—ultimately, legislation is the best answer for this thing. This is a step towards it as an incentive to—in the markets that we are having to go to for these investors for them to, I think, more realistically or more honestly or openly want to look at investments in those areas outside the gateway cities in the major States.

Mr. LABRADOR. So you mention it needs to be done through legislation, and we have been working on legislation to improve the program. What more can be done to ensure that these rural and true high unemployment areas are able to attract investors?

Mr. WALLS. I think I mentioned in my statement, I think our concern has been there had a been a small group that—again, sorry, the microphone goes in and out—have a vested interest in the status quo. And, you know, when you talk about market, you are talking about—there is two markets you are talking about: There is the 10,000 visa market. And right now that is oversubscribed, that has been mentioned. And I think the issues that we are all concerned about is what pricing and how does that effect the overall market.

But you also have, certain parties, they are looking at the market is defined as the market that they have enjoyed for the history of the program. We understand that to be over 90 percent of investors are going a very select market, or very affluent, nondistressed area. And so invariably, whatever reforms happen, it is going to affect that market, and they certainly are vested to keep that from happening. We as a rural State admittedly would like to see more of that dispersed in other areas of the country, like Arkansas and Idaho.

Mr. LABRADOR. Okay. Thank you.

Mr. North, if we are going—so let's assume we are going to continue the investor program, and I understand you don't want to continue it, but if we do, what other changes would you recommend to actually accomplish the goal of attracting capital to rural and high unemployment areas?

Mr. NORTH. I would change the definition of where the money should be spent. And I am not happy with the thought that developers are going to figure this out and create, you know, their own maps as they have done. So I would make it a different definition, and I would make it—I would try to get something that would really push investment into rural and genuinely distressed areas, such as downtown Detroit.

Mr. LABRADOR. Okay. Ms. Brunner, you stated that both the proposed increasing investment amounts and the proposed changes to the definitions will have a negative impact on your ability to attract investors. Is it the combination of both changes that will impact investment or is the one change more likely than the other to have the negative impact?

Ms. BRUNNER. They will a work in concert, Congressman. The increased numbers don't seem to—well, they are tied to a CPI calculation going back to 1990. They don't seem to be tied to a supply-and-demand model where you would try and figure out at what price can you achieve the same demand, which is the question I would like this committee to ask and get answered. So that is a very serious concern. That will impact demand.

The second thing that will impact demand is the ability of projects to qualify. The arbitrary and capricious nature of the TEA—of the existing TEA definition and the proposed TEA definition do a disservice to the program. At minimum, I would invite the committee to explore what other definitions are used within the Federal Government. And in the absence of that, our preference is that you eliminate the TEA, allow identical investments in distressed and rural areas and other areas, create set-aside programs that properly incent the investors.

The only variable that investors seem to care about right now is time. And so what I would invite the committee to do is to explore what they can do to manipulate the time factor for investors. If you manipulate that factor, you can drive investment anywhere you want it to go.

Mr. LABRADOR. Okay. Thank you, I yield back.

Mr. KING. The gentleman from Idaho yields back his time.

And the chair would now recognize the gentleman from New York, Mr. Nadler.

Mr. NADLER. Thank you, Mr. Chairman.

Mr. Chairman, in less than 2 months in office, President Trump has issued two unconstitutional and immoral executive orders attempting to enact the Muslim and refugee ban, is reportedly considering ordering women separated from their children, has threatened to punish so-called sanctuary cities even though doing so will likely make those communities less safe, and has embarked on building an unnecessary and fiscally irresponsible wall across the southern border. In short, he has fundamentally reoriented our immigration policy toward one of exclusion based on fear and ignorance rather than adhering to our historic commitment of being a place of refuge based on the belief we are stronger as a nation because of those who come to our shores.

In light of this radical departure in Federal policy, it seems a bit incongruous for our first immigration hearing since the Trump administration began to be focused on the EB–5 investor visa program, a useful but relatively minor program that offers visas in exchange for significant economic investment in the United States.

I hope we will soon conduct oversight into President Trump's cruel and shortsighted immigration policies. In the meantime, since we have the opportunity to consider the EB–5 program today, I want to ask a few questions about that program.

Now, Ms. Brunner, some critics of the EB–5 program argue that certain regional centers are in effect gerrymandering census tracts in order to create targeted employment areas and take advantage of the lower investment criteria for TEAs. Do you believe that the proposed regulations and other proposed reforms account for the unique circumstances of major urban centers where a census tract may only consist of a block or two?

Ms. BRUNNER. No, I do not, Congressman.

Mr. NADLER. Could you elaborate?

Ms. BRUNNER. Sure. Urban areas—first of all, census tracts are designated by density of population. So, in a rural area, you may have a single census tract in Wyoming or another rural State that covers 20-plus miles, single census tract. In an urban area, you may have a census tract that covers maybe four, six blocks.

Mr. NADLER. In my area, you have a census tract that covers half a block.

Ms. BRUNNER. There you go. Exactly. Exactly to my point. So, when you use census tracts as a basis of designation, either it be 12 in California or the doughnut approach that is used in the current proposed regulations, you completely ignore any principle of economic development. It is completely unrelated, actually, to the purpose of the TEA designation, which is to determine unemployment. You really have to look at the area in a whole different light.

Now, the Federal Government does an excellent job of that. There has been a lot of thought through a number of agencies, USDA, HUD, a number of agencies, not to mention the State-level work that is done on—that has been done on enterprise zones in the past or the current designations or the rural designations that exist.

I would invite the committee to not reinvent the wheel and either lean on the work that has already been done so diligently by other agencies in the Federal Government or to eliminate the conversation.

As much as the conversation of TEA designation and gerrymandering has hijacked this committee and the entire reform conversation, I think the most responsible thing we can do is to eliminate the conversation and eliminate TEAs.

Mr. NADLER. What do you mean by "eliminate the conversation"?

Ms. BRUNNER. We need to go to a single investment tier, and we need to use set-asides.

Mr. NADLER. And let me just elaborate for a moment. Also, if the purpose of this is to generate employment in under—in low-income areas, basically, in high-unemployment areas, not only do you have the distortion here where a census tract can be half a block or a block or two, but does it also ignore the fact that, in an area like an urban area, like in New York, you may have Hudson Yard, very upscale development, half a mile away from a very depressed neighborhood where the workers live?

Ms. BRUNNER. Well, I am actually in favor of commuting patterns because I think that they demonstrate the actual reality of economic development in the United States, that people—the variable that Bureau of Labor Statistics and a number of other Federal agencies use is, what is the commute that people would endure to go to work? That is why high speed——

Mr. NADLER. What I am saying is that, if you are looking, you are saying, as the chairman implied when he was reading that ad—that ad from that development, Hudson Yards, he was implying that this is a very rich area; you are not going to help low-income people, unemployed people. But that area, that high-end development area, is half a mile from Harlem and less than a mile from the South Bronx, which are very depressed, low-income areas where workers live.

Ms. BRUNNER. That is right.

Mr. NADLER. In other words, by looking at this and not taking that into account, you are distorting the reality of the effect of the economic development here, which is to help, arguably, to help low-income workers who live nearby, albeit in a different census tract and, therefore, to gerrymander the census tracts to—not to master reality but to show the reality that the low-income workers are living—who are being aided are living near the development, that is not wrong.

Ms. BRUNNER. That is correct.

Mr. NADLER. You agree with that?

Ms. BRUNNER. I do.

Mr. NADLER. Okay. I see that my time has expired.

I yield back, thank you.

Mr. KING. I thank the gentleman from New York.

Now I recognize the gentleman from Texas, Mr. Gohmert.

Mr. GOHMERT. Thank you, Mr. Chair.

I appreciate the witnesses being here today.

Director Gambler, I understood you had commented about the vetting that occurs with those who want to invest in this EB–5 program. What kind of vetting goes on?

Ms. GAMBLER. So, as part of our work, Congressman, we did not get into a lot of details on the background check process. However, sir, I would be happy to get some followup information and get back to you and your office with much more detail.

Mr. GOHMERT. Well, obviously, from the comments here, the focus is in the EB–5 program, you know, getting financial investments in the United States. And that seems to be the focus of the State Department as well. Much more important that we get the price we have named for prostituting our own visas than it is to figure out whether these people are going to be good, moral, upstanding folks here in the United States. And although a colleague may call two executive orders unconstitutional and immoral, it doesn't make them so any more than the Supreme Court saying the Dred Scott decision was constitutional. It was constitutional. Calling it so one way or another does not make it so. And there is nothing immoral about a President trying to protect people.

It really is astounding. As I sit and listen—I was listening in the back as well. I mean, it really is like that story, you know, we are just haggling over price. We have established what you are. The United States is willing to sell its soul. How much are we going to get for the price of selling our souls?

I wasn't even aware of the EB–5 program until my sheriff let us know.

But here is part of the story: A former Mexican Government official wanted for embezzling millions was arrested in Texas this month, then promptly ordered released by the State Department. A day after pulling rank on Smith County law enforcement officials, the State Department rescinded the order, but Hector Hernandez Javier Villarreal was gone by then. Villarreal, the former Secretary Executive of the Tax Administration Service of Coahuila, Mexico, was arrested on charges in Mexico relating to an alleged scheme involving embezzling millions of dollars from the Mexican Government. He posted a $1 million cash bond, then got himself a U.S. visa and skipped town. Villarreal surfaced in Tyler, Texas, when he, his wife, Maria Botello, and another man were pulled over for a routine stop. "All we did was make a traffic stop; they didn't have a front license plate," Smith County sheriff, J.B. Smith told FOX News. Police were given permission to search the vehicle. They found $67,000 in cash and a shotgun. Anyway, he said Homeland Security officials had told his department Villarreal was a high-profile and wanted fugitive. "We placed them in jail on money-laundering charges, seized the vehicle and the money; ICE came, picked him up from our jail, took him to Dallas, and that is the last we have seen." Villarreal and Botello posted bond on February 6, were released in the custody of Homeland Security Immigration and Customs. They were taken to a Dallas detention center for deportation. That is when State Department intervened. Homeland Security officials called to tell him the Federal diplomatic agency had ordered Villarreal and his wife released.

And so, anyway, I don't know that they have ever been found, but it seemed pretty clear the focus was getting the money. And, once again, like has been talked about, this guy offered 500,000 to invest, and he got a visa very immediately. And what comes to mind is, how many people in the world have massive amount of money that was obtained from immoral or illegal purposes, and we in America seem to say, "we don't care how you obtained your money; you could have swindled it from the Mexican people, but we want you in America if you will put some of that cash where we tell you to put it, and we won't even be that particular about where we tell you to put it"?

So I am appalled at this program. You know, America has degenerated to the point that, you know, our soul is for sale, and now we have got to negotiate about how high of a price we want. Give us your tired, your energetic. We don't care. Give us your immoral, your degenerate. As long as they have got money, the message is we want them in America, and we will give them a visa to get their money. I think it is an immoral message to send to the world. It feeds the hatred that some have for America that we don't care about being moral and upright in America; we care about the all mighty dollar. I for one would like to see it stop.

I yield back.

Mr. KING. The gentleman from Texas has yielded back.

The chair now recognizes the gentleman from Louisiana, Mr. Johnson.

Mr. JOHNSON of Louisiana. Thank you, Mr. Chairman.

Director Gambler, this is a couple for you. We are all committed to rooting out fraud, waste, and abuse, and I thank you for your commitment to that and your important work on it, all of you, for helping on that.

Just three quick questions on that topic. When the GAO was conducting its review to the proposed project investments in the targeted employment areas, was the information you were seeking easily accessible when you were trying to understand how the EB–5 recipients were actually investing this money?

Ms. GAMBLER. We specifically looked at files that were submitted in the fourth quarter of fiscal year 2015. That was a sample that was readily available for our review. It did require us to go through paper files for the 200 sample files that we looked at.

Mr. JOHNSON of Louisiana. So, of the sample files, did you find that it was clear and concise? I mean, it was easily understood where the money went and how they created jobs?

Ms. GAMBLER. We were able to get the data for our review out of the files. I would add, though, that some of the files can be thousands of pages long. And one of the key challenges with the program that we have pointed out in our work is the lack of data being readily available in an electronic format that allows for the agency to do things like identify fraud risks, look at trends in the program, that kind of thing.

Mr. JOHNSON of Louisiana. So is the need for additional information, or just is it a formatting issue to make it more readily accessible?

Ms. GAMBLER. In part, it is having the information available in such a way that it can be searched and utilized more easily for the purposes of like risk assessment and other things. USCIS is working toward a case management system, and so they are making some progress there, and that is a good and important step.

Mr. JOHNSON of Louisiana. So do we know when the case management system will be completed or released? Is there a target date for that?

Ms. GAMBLER. USCIS, I believe, was hoping to get something underway this fiscal year. We would be happy to follow up with them and get back to your office if that time frame has changed.

Mr. JOHNSON of Louisiana. I am just curious. I mean, we are all interested in increasing transparency, and the more that we can make it readily available and accessible, understandable for, you know, just taxpayers, the better, I think because we want to know, really, where all this money is going and how it is being spent, obviously.

Is the completion of the case management system, is that a—do you think it is a funding issue, or is it just timing; it is on their things-to-do list?

Ms. GAMBLER. At the point in time that we were doing our work last year, I think they were figuring out, kind of, what the parameters would be for that, what the requirements would be. So I think it is more just that they have to go through the process of determining what their requirements are and what type of system will meet their needs.

Mr. JOHNSON of Louisiana. Have you given them feedback or ideas on what will make it easier for you when you went through this process?

Ms. GAMBLER. Not specifically as it involves to a case management system related to the EB–5 program. But, more broadly, I think, as you are probably aware, USCIS relies on a paper-based process for adjudicating immigration benefit applications, and they are working through their transformation program to move to a more electronic system. And we have made a host of recommendations to the USCIS on that broader transformation effort designed to help them implement that program on a more effective basis.

Mr. JOHNSON of Louisiana. All right. Thank you.

I appreciate all of you being here.

Thank you.

Mr. KING. The gentleman from Louisiana returns his time.

And this concludes today's hearing. I want to thank all of our witnesses for your testimony here today and your response to all the questions of the panel.

Without objection, all members will have 5 legislative days to submit additional written questions for the witnesses or additional materials for the record.

This hearing is now adjourned.

○